Music

Therapy

Music
Therapy

written by
Alaric Lewis, O.S.B.

illustrated by
R.W. Alley

ONE
CARING
PLACE
Abbey Press

Text © 2001 by Alaric Lewis, O.S.B.
Illustrations © 2001 by St. Meinrad Archabbey
Published by One Caring Place
Abbey Press
St. Meinrad, Indiana 47577

Library of Congress Catalog Number
2001093039

ISBN 0-87029-356-7

Printed in the United States of America

Foreword

"If music be the food of love, play on," wrote William Shakespeare in *Twelfth Night*. And linking music with food and love is just another example of the Bard's genius. Music, after all—like food—has the ability to fill us, to satisfy those parts of our souls that hunger to express joy, longing, regret, sadness, sheer delight. And, like love, music has the ability to touch our hearts, to make us aware of people and places and events that have permanently imprinted themselves in our lives with melodies both sweet and sad.

This little book is written for anyone for whom music is a part of life. It offers reflections and guides to unlock the melodies that are part of life's composition, and to celebrate those sounds with thanksgiving in our hearts and a tune on our lips.

So, whether we're Pavarotti performing Puccini, or a soapy singer of shower show tunes; whether we want to mellow out with Mozart or samba with Santana; whether our pitch is precise and perfect or frustratingly flat—none of it matters. What matters is that to be really human is to appreciate music of all kinds; it ultimately helps us to know just how connected we all are. Play on, indeed!

1.

Birds sing, crickets chirp, children giggle—some of life's most beautiful music comes from instruments such as these. Let the ears of your heart be open to life's simple symphonies.

2.

A key element of any piece of music is its unique rhythm. We, too, possess our own unique rhythms that we feel deep in our hearts. Don't be afraid to march to your own beat—your music is just as beautiful as anyone else's!

3.

Although there exists in music the mournful sound of the cello, or the solemn resonance of a pipe organ, there is also the craziness of the kazoo, the whimsy of the slide whistle. Celebrate the quirkiness of life's music, realizing that it too is an important part of the whole symphony.

4.

Not everyone may appreciate our style of music, and they may want to turn a deaf ear to us or even shut us up. If we strive to really listen to one another, however, we might just find that our music can sound pretty good together.

5.

There are times when it seems
the world around us is nothing
but a dissonant cacophony of
painful noise. One act of
kindness or beauty, however,
can soar above the clamor
like a sweet symphony.

6.

Some people can make the
angels weep with joy at the
sound of their singing; others
can make them run for cover.
Regardless of how melodic the
voice, singing a little every day
helps put us in touch with the
great song of creation.

7.

Some music makes us sadly mindful of a loved one who is no longer with us. Even in the sadness, don't be afraid to hum along; for in so doing, we realize that their song continues in us.

8.

A baby's contented coo and hair-raising cry come from the same place. Even though we might not always like the music life plays for us, we can appreciate that the instruments used are beautiful, indeed.

9.

Many mothers and fathers sing gentle lullabies to their children to help bring about the peacefulness of slumber. Know that God desires to sing to us of such peace—that we may be lost in God's loving lullaby.

10.

Scattered throughout every piece
of music are rests, little breaks
from the sound to make us
appreciate the song all the more.
In the midst of life's harried
pace, recognize the sheer beauty
of silence, and enjoy its rests.

11.

Some of language's most beautiful words are set to melodies that can so combine with the text that nothing short of inspiration occurs. Pick up an old hymnal or songbook and belt out a favorite, feeling the amazing grace of such sweet sounds.

12.

Sometimes the smallest violin can soar above a full orchestra, begging you to pay attention to its plaintive pleading. Listen to the little voices in your life, and know they have something to sing about too.

13.

Sometimes a single voice can't be heard over the din of a busy world. But if we join our voices together in song, odds are good that not only will we be heard, but the world might just stand up and take note.

14.

When distance separates friends
from one another, music can
bring them closer. Listen to
an old song and think of good
times with friends with whom
you shared the music. You just
might find they seem as close as
the next beat.

15.

Sadness is a part of every life, and sometimes we need to experience it so that our joy may be more complete. Getting lost in a slow, reflective piece of music can help our hearts know that our sorrow is sometimes natural, and shared—not only with the composer—but with so many other listeners as well.

16.

Of course, staying sad for too long doesn't help anyone. Joyful music—from a rousing march to gentle laughter—helps complete the symphony, and makes us aware that dirges and songs of unbridled happiness use the same exact notes, just in different ways at different times.

17.

From a rousing pep-step song to a ponderous opus, certain music can inspire us to do things that we might want to put off. Hear in the urgency of each note the inspiration needed to tackle your next project.

18.

Russia produced Tchaikovsky;
Austria gave birth to Mozart;
England formed John Lennon;
the United States saw the
development of Duke Ellington.
In a world where there is much
division, hear in the swells
of their music the way to
understanding. Imagine a
universal song of peace.

19.

Dissonance, loud cymbals, screeching voices, clanging gongs: sometimes music expresses an anger that can make us feel uncomfortable. But our anger can teach us something, if we're not afraid to listen to it.

20.

Even the best musician hits a wrong note every now and then. Embrace your mistakes, and hear in them the necessary prelude to the fuller, richer song of humanity.

21.

A popular song once began, "I'd like to teach the world to sing." Recognize the valuable lesson in your failures and successes, your hopes and disappointments. And don't be afraid to share your song with others, for everyone has something to learn.

22.

Music isn't always about performance, and life shouldn't be either. If we find we're trying too hard to sing tunes for the approval of others, we're missing out on the delight in songs just because they're ours.

23.

Deadlines, appointments, money concerns, family struggles: life is filled with one worry after another. But the soothing melody of a quiet sonata has the ability to drown out the clamor of worry. Revel in the sweet music of calm.

24.

Life is too short to get into a rut, to listen to the same music over and over again—even if the familiarity of it all can be a comfort. Listen to something new and exciting, and see in the surprises of the music the possibilities that can exist when we trust that what is to come can be good.

25.

As we listen to music, we notice that each note, each beat, is in relation to another; each chord relies on the interdependence of several notes. Hear in these strains the music of life itself, and celebrate your connection with others.

26.

As long as music has been around, so have love songs, as people have desired to express the beauty of their hearts to others. Don't be afraid to sing your song of love to the important people in your life.

27.

Anger and hurt can at times
swell up in us so greatly
that we cannot seem to hear
anything else. Know that in
the words, "I forgive you,"
exists a harmony so sweet
that nothing can overcome it.

28.

Some people have no rhythm;
others sing off-key; still others
don't know a crescendo from a
credenza. When we begin to
think that we are the sum of
what we can (and can't) do,
we need realize that the
marvelous music of life itself
flows through our veins,
making all of us maestros.

29.

Composers go over the same sections of music time and time again to make sure they're just right, but eventually have to trust that the notes will do their magic. In life's composition, don't be afraid to try to tweak the music here and there, but also know when it's time to be at peace with what cannot be changed.

30.

Even the world's greatest composers had their critics, people who just didn't like the music they wanted to share. Know that critics will assail our music from time to time, but also know that that doesn't make the music—or us— any less beautiful.

31.

The greatest musical composers
and performers will tell you that
true greatness comes from much
discipline and practice.
Recognize that the never-ending
struggles of life are necessary
exercises—scales that help us
make life's music all the more
beautiful.

32.

Music has the ability to tap into our moods—whatever they may be. Listen to your heart, and don't be afraid of the beat that is there. Never be ashamed of the music that is in your soul.

33.

When life seems rocky, roll right over those rocks. A rolling stone gathers no moss, and if we keep on rockin', troubles will not cling to us either.

34.

It takes two to tango. Know that there are going to be times when we can't do it alone. In these times, grab on to a friend, listen to the beat, and dance up a storm—together.

35.

Everybody gets the blues sometimes; it's part of life's music. Even if there's no sun up in the sky for us right now, know that the stormy weather won't last.

Line up here for PARADE

36.

We all have things we know we should do, but sometimes we just can't work up the energy to face the music. While it's OK to put some things off, sometimes we have to just "step high and march," or the parade will pass us by.

37.

Some people treat music like a science: a precise, carefully orchestrated system of tones and rhythms that follow immutable laws. But music—and life—aren't always so standard. So we shouldn't be afraid to jazz it up every now and then.

38.

When listening to our favorite
music, we trust that each note
following each note will add up
to make something beautiful.
Know that you are God's most
amazing composition, soulfully
beautiful in your very self.

Alaric Lewis, O.S.B., is a Benedictine monk and Choirmaster of Saint Meinrad Archabbey in southern Indiana. He is also an associate editor at One Caring Place, Abbey Press Publications. He is the author of *PrayerStarters in Times of Pain or Illness* and *A Healing Year: Daily Meditations for Living With Loss*.

Illustrator for the Abbey Press Elf-help Books, **R.W. Alley** also illustrates and writes children's books. He lives in Barrington, Rhode Island, with his wife, daughter, and son.

The Story of the Abbey Press Elves

The engaging figures that populate the Abbey Press "elf-help" line of publications and products first appeared in 1987 on the pages of a small self-help book called *Be-good-to-yourself Therapy*. Shaped by the publishing staff's vision and defined in R.W. Alley's inventive illustrations, they lived out author Cherry Hartman's gentle, self-nurturing advice with charm, poignancy, and humor.

Reader response was so enthusiastic that more Elf-help Books were soon under way, a still-growing series that has inspired a line of related gift products.

The especially endearing character featured in the early books—sporting a cap with a mood-changing candle in its peak—has since been joined by a spirited female elf with flowers in her hair.

These two exuberant, sensitive, resourceful, kindhearted, lovable sprites, along with their lively elfin community, reveal what's truly important as they offer messages of joy and wonder, playfulness and co-creation, wholeness and serenity, the miracle of life and the mystery of God's love.

With wisdom and whimsy, these little creatures with long noses demonstrate the elf-help way to a rich and fulfilling life.

Elf-help Books

...adding "a little character" and a lot
of help to self-help reading!

Stress Therapy	#20153
Making-sense-out-of-suffering Therapy	#20156
Get Well Therapy	#20157
Anger Therapy	#20127
Caregiver Therapy	#20164
Self-esteem Therapy	#20165
Take-charge-of-your-life Therapy	#20168
Everyday-courage Therapy	#20167
Peace Therapy	#20176
Friendship Therapy	#20174
Christmas Therapy (color edition) $5.95	#20175
Grief Therapy	#20178
Happy Birthday Therapy	#20181
Forgiveness Therapy	#20184
Keep-life-simple Therapy	#20185
Acceptance Therapy (color edition) $5.95	#20182
Acceptance Therapy	#20190
Keeping-up-your-spirits Therapy	#20195
Slow-down Therapy	#20203

One-day-at-a-time Therapy	#20204
Prayer Therapy	#20206
Be-good-to-your-marriage Therapy	#20205
Be-good-to-yourself Therapy (hardcover) $10.95	#20196
Be-good-to-yourself Therapy	#20255

Book price is $4.95 unless otherwise noted.
Available at your favorite giftshop or bookstore—
or directly from One Caring Place, Abbey Press
Publications, St. Meinrad, IN 47577.
Or call 1-800-325-2511.